ISBN- 9798865388784

Cover design by: Shari Howard
Library of Congress Control Number: 2018675309
Printed in the United States of America

CONTENTS

Copyright

Introduction

Preface

Chapter 1: Signing Agent 1

Chapter 2: Role of the Signing Agent 2

Chapter 3 Notary Public: 4

Chapter 4: Role of the Notary Public 5

Chapter 5: Signing Agents vs. Notaries 9

Chapter 6: Comparison 12

Chapter 7: The Final Verdict 14

Afterword 17

INTRODUCTION

Welcome to "Notary Public vs. Signing Agent-Which Title Carries More Weight?," a book crafted from years of experience and a genuine passion for notary work. I'm Shari Howard, a proud native of the Sunshine State, Florida. My journey in the world of notary services began in 2007, a time when notary work was just a spark of curiosity for me.

Starting with general notary work (GNW), I ventured through a multitude of companies and departments, learning the ropes and embracing the ever-evolving landscape of notarial responsibilities. The catalyst for writing this book was a simple question – a reminder that there are no 'stupid' questions in the quest for knowledge and improvement.

My goal with this book is to be your guiding light on your notary journey, whether you're considering it as a side hustle, a part-time gig, or even as the foundation for a full-fledged career. In a world with thousands of notaries and signing agents, always remember there's only one you. Embrace your uniqueness, and strive to be the best version of yourself in every room, even when it's packed with a million notaries and signing agents. Let's start on your journey together, and may this book enlighten your path to notary success.

PREFACE

In a world increasingly filled with complex legal documents, contracts, and financial transactions, Notary Publics and Signing Agents serve as vigilant protectors, quietly ensuring the documents we sign are legally sound and genuine. Yet, these roles are often entwined and misunderstood, and the distinctions between them aren't always crystal clear.

This book, "Notary Public vs. Signing Agent- Which Title Carries More Weight?," aims to uncover the true nature of these two essential professions. Through a journey of exploration and revelation, we will discuss the unique roles of Notaries and Signing Agents, interpret the subtleties of their titles, and engage in the discussions that revolve around these critical roles.

For those who have ever found themselves confused for one when they are the other or have been fascinated by the nuances of these roles, this book is your guide. I welcome you to join me on this journey to understand the differences, recognize the shared aspects, and become part of the ongoing conversations that envelop these pivotal professions.

CHAPTER 1: SIGNING AGENT

A signing agent is a specialized professional who plays a pivotal role in facilitating the signing of important documents. These individuals act as neutral witnesses during the signing process, ensuring that documents are executed accurately, signed by the correct parties, and notarized when necessary. The primary responsibility of a signing agent is to verify the identities of the signers, confirm that documents are complete and accurate, and oversee the signing process. They often work in various fields, including real estate, finance, legal, and more, to ensure the proper and legally binding execution of documents.

In the world of real estate, a signing agent often plays a crucial role in ensuring a smooth and legally compliant property transaction. Let's consider a scenario where a signing agent is involved:

Scenario:

John and Sarah are purchasing their first home. They've already been through the process of finding the perfect house, securing a mortgage loan, and completing various paperwork with their real estate agent and lender. Now, it's time for the closing, the point at which ownership of the property officially transfers to them.

CHAPTER 2: ROLE OF THE SIGNING AGENT

1. Verification: On the day of the closing, a signing agent arrives at the title company's office where the closing is taking place. Their first role is to verify the identities of John and Sarah. They will ask for government-issued identification to confirm that they are indeed the buyers.

2. Document Review: The signing agent carefully reviews all the documents related to the real estate transaction. This includes the mortgage documents, the deed of trust, the promissory note, and other legal agreements. The signing agent ensures that all documents are correctly filled out and that they match the terms agreed upon by the buyers and the lender.

3. Notarization: When required, the signing agent notarizes specific documents. For instance, they may notarize the deed of trust, which provides a legal record of the mortgage, adding an extra layer of authentication to the document.

4. Witnessing Signatures: The signing agent witnesses John and Sarah signing all the necessary documents. They ensure that each document is signed in the right places and that the signatures are consistent with the identification provided.

5. Finalizing the Closing: Once all the documents are properly signed, the signing agent helps coordinate the exchange of funds, including the down payment and any closing costs. They make sure that these financial aspects are handled securely and in accordance with the transaction terms.

In this scenario, the signing agent's role is vital in ensuring that the real estate closing process proceeds without any hitches and that all legal requirements are met. They play a key role in protecting the interests of both the buyers and the lender while making the real estate transaction legally binding.

CHAPTER 3 NOTARY PUBLIC:

A Notary Public is a public officer appointed by the state government, authorized to act as an impartial witness in the execution of various legal documents. The role of a Notary Public is broader in scope compared to that of a signing agent. Notaries have the authority to acknowledge signatures, administer oaths, and certify or notarize documents. This includes verifying the authenticity of the signers' identities, administering oaths or affirmations, and placing their official seal on documents to attest to their legality and authenticity. Notaries ensure the documents' compliance with state laws and regulations.

Notarization Of A Legal Document:

Notaries Public often find themselves in various situations where their services are needed for notarizing important documents. Let's consider a scenario where a Notary Public is involved:

Scenario:

Amy is starting her own business and needs to sign a partnership agreement with her co-founder, Tom. This partnership agreement outlines the terms, responsibilities, and legal aspects of their business venture.

CHAPTER 4: ROLE OF THE NOTARY PUBLIC

1. Appointment Setup: Amy schedules an appointment with a local Notary Public to notarize the partnership agreement. She must ensure that all parties involved, including Tom and the Notary Public, are present at the scheduled time.

2. Identification Verification: At the meeting, the Notary Public verifies the identities of Amy and Tom by examining their government-issued identification documents, such as driver's licenses or passports. This step ensures that the right individuals are signing the document.

3. Oath or Affirmation: The Notary Public administers an oath or affirmation to Amy and Tom, which requires them to truthfully affirm that the contents of the partnership agreement are accurate and that they understand the legal implications of the document.

4. Document Notarization: The Notary Public places their official seal and signature on the partnership agreement. This action certifies that the document has been properly executed and that the signatures are genuine. The notarization adds an extra layer of authenticity and legality to the document.

5. Recording and Record-Keeping: The Notary Public records the notarization in their official notary journal, which serves as a legal record of the notarial act. They maintain this journal for documentation and verification purposes.

6. Completion and Finalization: Once the document is notarized, it is considered legally binding and authenticated. Amy and Tom

can now proceed with their business venture, confident that the partnership agreement is legally valid.

In this scenario, the Notary Public's role is to act as an impartial witness to the signing of the partnership agreement, ensuring that the document's execution meets legal requirements and that the parties involved understand the document's implications. The notarization process provides an added level of credibility and legal assurance to the document.

If an individual is well-versed in both general notary work and loan closing documents, they could reasonably consider themselves capable of functioning as both a Notary Public and a signing agent. General notary work involves the authentication of signatures and documents, and having expertise in this area is fundamental for both roles. In addition to basic notarization tasks, signing agents specifically focus on loan closing documents. Being proficient in these documents, which are a critical component of real estate and financial transactions, is a key aspect of a signing agent's responsibilities. Therefore, someone familiar with both notarial procedures and the complexities of loan documents can effectively carry out the tasks of both roles.

One might argue that a notary and a signing agent are one and the same due to the overlap in some of their responsibilities. Both professionals deal with the authentication of signatures, verification of identities, and the certification of documents. Moreover, they often work in related fields, such as real estate, where the roles can become intertwined. In real estate transactions, for instance, a signing agent is frequently required to notarize documents to ensure their legal validity, blurring the lines between the two roles. However, it's important to note that while there is some overlap, a Notary Public has a broader mandate and can notarize a wide range of documents beyond those typically handled by a signing agent, who primarily focuses on overseeing the signing of specific transaction-related documents. Therefore, while there are similarities, they are distinct roles with varying scopes of authority and specialization.

One example of a state that has specific educational requirements and courses for certified signing agents is California. As of my last knowledge update in September 2021, California has a comprehensive process for becoming a certified notary public and a certified loan signing agent.

To become a certified loan signing agent in California, individuals are typically required to complete the following steps:

1. Become a Notary Public: First, you must become a commissioned Notary Public in California. This involves passing an exam and completing an approved education course.
2. Loan Signing Courses: Once you are a commissioned notary, you can then take specific courses related to loan signing, which cover the intricacies of loan documents, real estate transactions, and notarization procedures for loan documents.
3. Background Check: You may be required to undergo a background check as part of your certification.
4. Exam: After completing the necessary coursework, you might need to pass an exam to demonstrate your understanding of the loan signing process.
5. Certification: Once you've successfully completed the steps above, you can be certified as a loan signing agent in California, allowing you to handle loan document signings, particularly in the real estate industry.

Please note that the requirements and regulations in California, as well as in other states, may have evolved since my last update in September 2021. It's essential to check with the California Secretary of State's office or the relevant regulatory body to obtain the most current information on the specific requirements for becoming a certified signing agent in the state.

Furthermore, the ability to understand the nuances of loan closing documents and apply notarial practices in this context is highly advantageous. It allows for a comprehensive approach to handling real estate and financial transactions, ensuring that documents are not only properly signed and executed but also notarized in compliance with relevant laws and regulations. By combining these skill sets, an individual can offer a broader range of services, increasing their value to clients and becoming a versatile professional in the field of document authentication and legal compliance.

CHAPTER 5: SIGNING AGENTS VS. NOTARIES

There are two roles that often overlap but come with distinct responsibilities and income structures: signing agents and notaries. In this chapter, we'll dig a little into what you should know about these two roles and the critical differences between them.

Signing agents are instrumental in the complex world of real estate transactions. They are usually hired by title companies to handle the crucial finalization of real estate deals. Here's what you need to know:

Document Preparation: A significant part of a signing agent's role involves preparing the necessary closing documents for the signing day. They ensure that all documents are accurate and ready for signatures.

Client Meetings: Signing agents meet clients at the title company's office or another preferred location for the signers. This is often done to guide the clients through the signing process and answer any questions they might have.

Document Oversight: Once the documents are signed, the signing agent must carefully review them to ensure they are executed correctly. This step is crucial to maintain the integrity of the transaction.

Document Handling: The signing agent is responsible for sending a copy of the signed documents to the title company and mailing the originals promptly to the loan servicer. This helps ensure the documents reach the appropriate parties in a timely manner.

Payment: Payment for signing agents varies. Some receive payment immediately from the title company, while others are paid on a monthly basis. The payment typically ranges from $50 to $250 per signing, regardless of the number of signatures required.

* * *

Notaries: The General Notary Work

As a notary, you are more inclined to engage in general notary work, often referred to as GNW. This encompasses a wide range of notarial duties, from notarizing affidavits to wills and trusts. Key points to consider include:

Notarial Fees: Depending on your state, you can charge a maximum fee per notarization. For example, in Florida, the maximum fee is $10 per notarization. If a document requires multiple notarizations, you can charge accordingly.

Additional Charges: In addition to the notarization fee, you can charge for travel or mileage if you need to go to your client. This can add to your earnings.

Versatility: Notaries have the flexibility to notarize various documents, including single-owner deeds, which might require only one notarization.

Income Potential: Being a notary can be lucrative, and it doesn't involve as much driving or supplies as signing agent work.

* * *

Balancing Both Roles: The Work Is The Same

One intriguing aspect is that you can wear both hats in a single day if you choose. Ultimately, whether you brand yourself as a signing agent or a notary depends on your client base and marketing strategy. The work, at its core, remains the same - ensuring the legal execution of documents.

Beware Of Misleading Courses And Promises

Yes, there is an abundance of courses and promises of high earnings. Be cautious when considering these. In many states, signing agent training is not required, but notary training is often free. Spending exorbitant amounts on signing agent courses can be questionable. Be sure to ask for proof of actual earnings from signing agent work rather than course sales.

Conclusion: Making Informed Choices

In this business, logical decisions and asking questions are your best allies. Don't hesitate to investigate opportunities thoroughly, and if you feel you're being taken advantage of, report the company to your state's authorities. Remember, the key to success in the notary world is not in the title but in your commitment, knowledge, and ethical practice.

CHAPTER 6: COMPARISON

There can be a notable difference in pay between a signing agent and a traditional notary public due to the nature of their roles and the additional responsibilities of the signing agent. Signing agents often command higher fees because their job extends beyond basic notarization. They are required to meticulously oversee the signing of complex and extensive loan and real estate documents. Their role may also involve conducting "scan backs," where they scan the signed documents and ensure their accuracy before mailing the originals off to a designated location, typically at a FedEx office. This meticulous process adds an extra layer of assurance in ensuring the documents are complete and error-free. In contrast, a traditional notary public typically notarizes documents and provides them back to the requester on the spot, without the additional responsibilities associated with

thorough review, scan backs, and mailing of documents. This difference in responsibilities and the level of expertise required is often reflected in the compensation, making signing agents generally earn more than traditional notaries for their specialized and comprehensive services.

While both signing agents and Notaries Public are involved in witnessing and verifying documents, there are key differences between them. Notaries Public have a broader authority to notarize various legal documents, administer oaths, and certify signatures, which may extend beyond the scope of signing agents. Signing agents, on the other hand, are specialized professionals focused primarily on overseeing the signing of specific documents, often in industries like real estate and finance. They ensure the correctness of documents and may or may not be Notaries Public themselves. Notaries Public have a more general role in legal matters, whereas signing agents have a more specific and transaction-focused role.

CHAPTER 7: THE FINAL VERDICT

In the world of notary work and signing agents, it might seem like there's a distinction between the two roles. But, if you ask me, they are essentially one and the same. Why? Well, let's dive into the basics and break it down.

First things first, you can't be a signing agent without being a notary. It's like trying to run before you can walk. To put it simply, becoming a notary is your first step, and from there, you can expand your horizons by taking on signing agent responsibilities. So, how can you call yourself a signing agent if you're not a notary? The short answer: you can't.

Let me share a true story with you that helped solidify my belief in this unity. After I passed my exam and officially became a certified signing agent, I excitedly sent a mass text to all my realtor friends to share my achievement. To my surprise, one of them responded with, "What's a signing agent?" In that moment, I eagerly explained what a signing agent does and all the responsibilities that come with the title.

However, her response caught me off guard. She simply said, "Oh, so you're just a notary?" It left me pondering the distinctions, or rather the lack thereof. From that day forward, I realized that there wasn't really much of a difference. It became clear as I reflected on the documents I had notarized. They often indicated that a notary and a signing agent were essentially the same thing.

In my eyes, the main role of a signing agent is to ensure that the buyers fully grasp the terms of the loan they are undertaking. On the other hand, a notary is, in essence, an uninterested third party. This is important because it provides a layer of impartiality. In case any issues or disputes arise, the mortgage company can claim that they hired a "signing agent" who is not on their payroll but was brought in as an external professional.

Now, here's the key takeaway – whether you choose to call yourself a notary or a signing agent, it's all about how you want to market yourself. These roles are interconnected, and you can describe your work in whichever way resonates with you and your clients. Ultimately, your passion and dedication to your work will shine through, no matter how you choose to word it. In this journey, let's embrace the unity of notaries and signing agents, and always remember that your commitment and professionalism make the difference, not just the title you use.

AFTERWORD

In wrapping up this book, I'm compelled to address a fundamental question that you, the reader, may be pondering: What distinguishes a notary from a signing agent and which title carries more significance?

Throughout the pages preceding this afterword, you've been exposed to the practicalities, responsibilities, and the nuanced world of notaries and signing agents. You've delved into the core of these professions, both of which are integral to the world of notarization and document signing.

Your exploration has unveiled the common ground and distinctions that exist between these roles. It's important to note that a title alone doesn't define the importance of what one does. The value in these roles comes from their expertise, ethics, and dedication to ensuring the validity of documents.

While this book aimed to shed light on the differences, it's crucial to remember that the significance of your work lies in the commitment to professionalism, adherence to legal standards, and the trust of those who rely on your services.

Ultimately, whether you don the title of notary or signing agent, the impact you make in this field is a testament to your dedication and the trust you've earned from your clients. Continue to explore, question, and expand your knowledge, because it's not the title that carries weight; it's the quality of your work and the difference you make that truly matters.

Thank you for joining me on this journey of discovery and professional growth.

Shari Howard
October 26, 2023